MW00933798

George R. Moscone Elementary
2576 HARRISON ST.
SAN FRANCISCO, CA 94110-2720
PHONE # (415) 695-5736
FAX # (415) 695-5341

IT'S A PENGUIN!

by Kerry Dinmont

BUMBA BOOKS™

LERNER PUBLICATIONS ◆ MINNEAPOLIS

Note to Educators:

Throughout this book, you'll find critical thinking questions. These can be used to engage young readers in thinking critically about the topic and in using the text and photos to do so.

Copyright © 2019 by Lerner Publishing Group, Inc.

All rights reserved. International copyright secured. No part of this book may be reproduced, stored in a retrieval system, or transmitted in any form or by any means—electronic, mechanical, photocopying, recording, or otherwise—without the prior written permission of Lerner Publishing Group, Inc., except for the inclusion of brief quotations in an acknowledged review.

Lerner Publications Company
A division of Lerner Publishing Group, Inc.
241 First Avenue North
Minneapolis, MN 55401 USA

For reading levels and more information, look up this title at www.lernerbooks.com.

Library of Congress Cataloging-in-Publication Data

Names: Dinmont, Kerry, 1982– author.
Title: It's a penguin! / Kerry Dinmont.
Description: Minneapolis : Lerner Publications, [2019] | Series: Bumba books. Polar animals | Audience: Age 4–7. | Audience: K to Grade 3. | Includes bibliographical references and index.
Identifiers: LCCN 2018003767 (print) | LCCN 2018002340 (ebook) | ISBN 9781512482874 (eb pdf) | ISBN 9781512482836 (lb : alk. paper) | ISBN 9781541526952 (pb : alk. paper)
Subjects: LCSH: Penguins—Juvenile literature.
Classification: LCC QL696.S473 (print) | LCC QL696.S473 D56 2019 (ebook) | DDC 598.47--dc23

LC record available at https://lccn.loc.gov/2018003767

Manufactured in the United States of America
1 – CG – 7/15/18

30723000125857

Table of
Contents

Penguins Swim

Penguins are birds.

They have wings.

But they cannot fly.

Emperor penguins live

in Antarctica.

They are the

largest penguins.

Penguins are good swimmers.

Their wings help them swim.

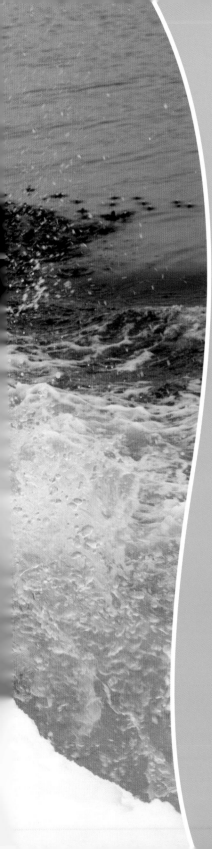

Penguins eat fish and other

sea animals.

They dive deep in the ocean

for their prey.

Thick feathers keep a penguin warm.

Penguins also huddle in groups

for warmth.

Why do you think huddling in groups keeps penguins warm?

A female penguin lays one egg in winter.

Then she leaves the group to hunt.

The male stays with the egg.

He keeps it warm.

He warms the egg for weeks.

egg

The female returns, and the

chick hatches.

The female feeds the chick.

The male leaves to hunt.

The female keeps the chick warm.

Chicks start to hunt in summer.

How do you think a mother penguin warms her chick?

Parts of a Penguin

feathers

wing

claws

Picture Glossary

dive

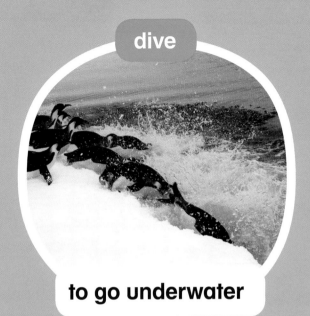

to go underwater

hatches

breaks out
of an egg

huddle

to gather
in a group

prey

an animal that is
hunted and eaten
by other animals

23

Read More

Boothroyd, Jennifer. *From Egg to Penguin*. Minneapolis: Lerner Publications, 2017.

Esbaum, Jill. *Penguins*. Washington, DC: National Geographic Society, 2014.

Salomon, David. *Penguins!* New York: Random House, 2017.

Index

Photo Credits

The images in this book are used with the permission of: © KeithSzafranski/iStock.com, pp. 5, 18, 23 (top right); © VargaJones/iStock.com, pp. 6–7; © Christopher Michel, p. 9; © Iurii Kazakov/Shutterstock.com, pp. 10–11, 23 (top left); © polarman/Shutterstock.com, pp. 13, 23 (bottom right); © Stu Shaw/Shutterstock.com, p. 14; © Wolfgang Kaehler/Superstock/Glow Images, p. 17; © vladsilver/Shutterstock.com, p. 21; © Jan Martin Will/Shutterstock.com, p. 22; © Allexxandar/Shutterstock.com, p. 23 (bottom right).

Front Cover: © Roger Clark ARPS/Shutterstock.com.